MILITARY UNIFORMS
THE SPLENDOUR OF THE PAST

With an introduction by Lt-Col J B R Nicholson

ORBIS BOOKS
LONDON

Contents

Colour photographs by: Bibliothèque Nationale/Snark: 34, 103; Gunn Brinson: 116, 117; British Museum/Photo Fleming: 70; Bulloz/Versailles: 1, 2, 19, 20; Giraudon: 14; Su Gooders/Guildhall: 4, 11; India Office Library/Photo Fleming: 61, 66; Mansell Collection: 28; Mas/Archivo Hist. Militar, Madrid: 44, 53, 58; Museo del Risorgimento, Milan: 57; National Army Museum: 16, 38, 39, 41, 47, 63, 64, 67, 79, 81, 104, 109–113, 115; National Army Museum/Photo Chris Barker: 90, 91; Lt-Col J B R Nicholson: 3, 5, 17, 23–27, 33, 35–37, 42, 43, 45, 46, 48, 50, 54, 56, 62, 65, 71, 72, 74–78, 80, 83, 85, 88, 93–97, 100–102, 105–108; Col Nicholson/ A C Cooper: 22, 29; Parker Gallery: 29, 52, 82, 86, 89, 92, 114; Scala/Bertarelli: 59; Scala/Museo del Risorgimento, Milan: 55; Scala/Palazzo Carignano, Turin: 60; Scala/Palazzo del Municipio, Trento: 40; Staatsbibliothek Berlin: 15, 49, 51, 69; Tallandier: 6–10. 12, 13, 18, 21, 30–32, 68, 84, 87; Victoria & Albert Museum: 73; Oska Wood/Tallandier: 118–120.
By gracious permission of Her Majesty Queen Elizabeth II, Windsor Castle/Photo A C Cooper: 98.

© Istituto Geografico de Agostini, Novara 1973
English edition © Orbis Publishing Limited, London 1973
Phototypeset in England by Petty and Sons Ltd, Leeds
Printed in Italy by IGDA, Novara
ISBN 0 85613 136 9

War has never been a pleasant business, although in many countries it was considered the only worthwhile occupation for a man, and in others the only suitable career for the upper class. The mystique of the noble warrior facing death with a smile dies hard, but except in the case of the Spanish matador it is no longer deemed necessary to dress in one's best for the occasion. The fighting man has long since reserved his best for formal or social functions, preferring to meet death in the more humble and informal attire known as battle dress. In fact, one of the objects of battle dress is to avoid or at least postpone this very meeting, and so the 'pomp and panoply' of war has vanished from the field of battle.

The study of military uniform is more than a mere analysis of contemporary costume, to which, according to period, it may or may not conform. Apart from cut and colouring, the silhouette of fashion, the quirk of nationality in the adaptation of some widespread pattern, much militaria may be classed as an art form in its own right, and has an intrinsic value of its own bearing no relation to money. The rules of heraldry, the classic principles of design, the fine art of the tailor and the virtuosity of the embroiderer (at times astonishing) are but some aspects of this subject. Great Britain and its forces are fortunate in having an unrivalled variety, for whilst other nations rationalized their uniforms, and units often varied by no more than a numeral, the British units maintained every possible regimental difference to the last ditch.

In a book of this size it is only possible to skim over the surface of a subject in which the weight of known detail would sink a battleship, but in which there are still large areas far from adequately documented. I aim no higher than to awaken the reader's interest in the subject.

The choice of illustrations is always difficult; there are always so many one would wish to include. The growing interest in military costume and accoutrements is one of the phenomena of our times, and the high demand has so forced up prices that the average collector can no longer hope to acquire good original material on a modest budget, as was once possible. Failing the original a good reproduction is the next best thing for purposes of study. I have, therefore, tried to use contemporary material wherever possible, preferring a naive contemporary print to a modern reconstruction, however good. An artist has the feel of his own period of history, the time at which he lives, and this comes out in his work. The human figure may be stylised to conform with the artistic ideals of his time, but this seems to me to be valid; the possibly unconscious 'modernizing' effect of a later artist, rendering a subject in the idiom of his own period, does not.

German dragoon (heavy cavalryman) of the 'Second Reich'
(1871–1918)

The Revolutionary Wars

Between 1789 and 1792 the French nation dissolved into the chaos of revolution and Europe entered upon a period of immense military activity, a period which was to see the formal well-drilled formations of the *Ancien Régime* overthrown by the enthusiasm of a rabble in arms.

By the end of the eighteenth century, the general pattern of military costume for regular troops was much the same throughout Europe in both infantry and cavalry – the cut-away tail coat revealing the waistcoat, gaiters, a cocked hat, and formally dressed and powdered hair. The skirts had dummy turnbacks, vestigial remnants of the full skirts which, for convenience, were turned and buttoned back to allow freer movement of the legs. History was to repeat itself in the French Army, immortalized in *Beau Geste* and other romantic tales of the Foreign Legion. The waistcoat was sleeved and used as an undress garment for drills and fatigues. The gaiter was in almost universal use, long white ones being favoured for formal wear in most armies, although the British had gone into black earlier in the century, and reduced them to knee length except in the Guards, who retained the long white ones for parade. The cocked hat was ubiquitous, and often worn by those units which normally sported a special headdress, such as hussars or light dragoons when off duty or walking out, and even upon some parades as an alternative to the full dress headdress. The queuing and powdering of hair, with pomatum and powder for officers and tallow and flour for other ranks, continued into the next century, although the 'windswept' look popularized by the neo-classical movement soon ousted it. (The style still survives on the heads of the British Counsel in court, although British judges wear wigs of an older fashion.)

Heavy cavalry wore top boots, often with a sort of canvas knee guard to protect the clothing, which may be seen above the boot top giving the appearance of gaiters worn under the boot. Light cavalry tended to wear lighter boots, and hussars had a special design of their own. The Russians were at this time experimenting with a new concept in uniforms and military dress, which included the abolition of pigtails and hair powder; it was so eminently practical that it was doomed to failure, and was soon abandoned in favour of a style more in keeping with contemporary military thinking. Curiously enough, the headdress of this experimental costume survived on the heads of the Horse Grenadiers of the Russian Imperial Guard until 1914.

Needless to say there were exceptions to these basic trends, some nations having their own developments, such as the mitre caps of Prussian grenadiers and the bearskin of British grenadiers, both developing along different lines from a common origin. In one the mitre cap became formalised with a die-stamped metal front, in the other it disappeared under a blanket of fur. There was, of course, a wide selection of national costumes adapted for war and formalised into uniforms, such as those worn by the Scottish Highlander, the Hungarian hussar, the Polish lancer, or the Greek *evzone*.

Cavalry uniforms

The first type of cavalry was the 'heavies', mounted on large horses. These horses were preferably black, but this breed, the war or 'great' horse of earlier times, was dying out. The dragoons or medium-weight cavalry were mounted on lighter horses. These dragoons tended to lose their ability to function as infantry when dismounted, owing to a psychological desire to upgrade themselves to cavalry proper and to shed the rather 'infra dig' infantry connotation. (It is interesting to note that such seventeenth century writers as Wallhausand included dragoons in their works on cavalry and not in those on infantry.) This caused something of a tactical hiatus which had later to be filled by such expedients as mounted infantry who were in fact dragoons in all save name. There were also various types of lighter cavalry with a variety of names, but all designed to undertake scouting and outpost duties, for which the 'heavies' were not considered suitable. In some countries they were simply called 'light horse' or 'light dragoons'

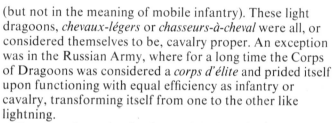

Above: Austro-Hungarian hussars. Right: British Guards officer

(but not in the meaning of mobile infantry). These light dragoons, *chevaux-légers* or *chasseurs-à-cheval* were all, or considered themselves to be, cavalry proper. An exception was in the Russian Army, where for a long time the Corps of Dragoons was considered a *corps d'élite* and prided itself upon functioning with equal efficiency as infantry or cavalry, transforming itself from one to the other like lightning.

Some armies maintained sartorially fully fledged hussars in full Hungarian dress, as in Russia, Prussia and France; but in Great Britain only a few specimens had been seen, such as the Duke of Cumberland's orderlies earlier in the century. For the last years of the century British light dragoons gravitated towards the hussar dress, although it was only officers who wore the slung pelisse. The wearing of the *mirliton* or *flügelmütze*, a tall conical cap of felt with a streamer, cords, tassels, and a plume increased the resemblance to foreign hussars – a resemblance which vanished in 1812, when a new uniform cut like that of Polish Lancers with a *shako* in lieu of the 'Tarleton helmet' was introduced. Incidentally the Tarleton helmet, named after its inventor in the American War of Independence, was beloved of British volunteers of the period. The introduction of this new uniform will serve to illustrate a common enough point. Although the regulations appeared in 1812, some regiments were still wearing the old-style uniform in 1815 at the Battle of Waterloo. Thus knowledge of the regulations in force at any given time is only the starting point in establishing what was worn at that date.

British Army dress

The hussar dress in all its glory, including the fur cap, was introduced in the first decade of the new century by the conversion of four regiments of light dragoons. Needless to say the introduction of a foreign style of dress came in for a great deal of criticism. Impractical it may have become; elegant it most certainly was. Its expense none can deny. It was estimated that General Sir Stapleton Cotton's hussar dress was worth 500 guineas as he stood, a very

considerable sum in a period when £40 per annum was considered a goodly fortune.

One thing is reasonably certain in the study of military costume: however rigid the regulations and however carefully they are worded, there are always exceptions and deviations which confound previous ideas. It might be thought that a copy of the appropriate dress regulations plus a sample or two of cloth, buttons and lace would provide all that is necessary to complete one's knowledge of a particular example. This is not so. The study of uniforms might be an exact science if obedience were universal; but conservative dislike of change, a love of traditional forms, a tailor's sense of fitness and changing contemporary fashion – together with plain bloody-mindedness – combine to denigrate the regulations.

The British Army and its derivatives had a special peculiarity in that without a direct order it was nearly impossible to get officers into uniform, and that if this was achieved they got out of it as soon as possible. Orders are full of the fulminations of general officers against such deviations as a tendency to sport a mixed military and civilian costume, presumably in the interests of comfort. In India, for example, in the very month in which the great Mutiny of the Bengal Army broke out, the General Officer commanding the Bombay Army found it necessary to issue an order 'peremptorily prohibiting' officers from wearing plain clothes (civilian clothing) on duty. This contrasts sharply with the Prussian and Russian services in which officers were seldom seen out of uniform. This was largely due to the social cachet bestowed by the right to wear uniform, and at the turn of this century wealthy young men were more than anxious to serve in the Guards regiments of the Russian Army without pay.

The informality of dress of the early Revolutionary armies, while doubtless reflecting a similar informality of outlook, was not entirely voluntary. It was due largely to difficulties of supply and lack of funds. However, there were those who managed to attain a standard of sartorial elegance which spread under the Directory (1795–1799) and which reached a peak of magnificence under the

Officers of Austro-Hungarian *Jäger* (riflemen)

Consulate (1799–1804) with the establishment of the Consular Guard. Once more France had a force of impeccably turned-out troops. Meanwhile the French expedition to Egypt (1798) familiarized Europe with some oriental novelties, notably the Mameluke sword and of course, the full Mameluke costume which was worn by those Mamelukes who were incorporated into the Guard by Napoleon, only to be massacred years later by the ignorant and suspicious *Marseillais.*

Countries and colours

By the end of the century the various nationalities had adopted generally accepted colours. The British were still famed for their scarlet, royal regiments having blue facings and gold lace; these three colours being the livery or heraldic colours of the Royal Arms. The infantry of the *Ancien Régime* and the Austrian Army wore white with various colour facings, the Prussians dark blue, and the Russians dark green. The word 'facing' refers to those parts of the uniform – collar, cuffs, piping, and so on – which were of a different colour to the main garment. Thus the French Swiss Guard wore red with dark blue facings and white lace. The French Napoleonic infantry did not have different colour facings for each regiment; the only difference was in the numeral on the cap plate. Riflemen tended to wear green, the colour favoured by the foresters and huntsmen from whom they had originally been raised by Frederick the Great. Cavalry tended to retain different facings for each regiment, and the hussars in particular were extremely showy.

The advantages of national colours from the point of recognition are manifest, and it must be remembered that black powder does not improve visibility on the battlefield.

The further advantages of standardization and bulk manufacture are obvious, although clothing by the colonel of the regiment who was allocated a fixed sum per head (and made what he could out of it sometimes), persisted in the British Army until well into the nineteenth century. Lord Cardigan, however, who led the Light Brigade at Balaclava, spent thousands of pounds a year from his own pocket on the mens' uniforms which he had made by West End tailors in London; he also purchased thoroughbred horses. This system of individual regimental arrangements persisted in the Silladar cavalry regiments of the Indian Army until the First World War, when it was found impossible to maintain the endless variety of regimental patterns, cloth and accoutrements in the field.

The Napoleonic wars saw the whole of Europe in arms and an unparalelled number of all nationalities in uniform. Apart from all the various national armies, there were French units serving with the British, Poles serving with Napoleon, others against him, German units on both sides and so on in a bewildering confusion; and since all had to have their own distinctive uniform if possible, the variety of military millinery was almost unlimited.

The paintings of Lejeune

In order to get a basic idea of costumes of the Napoleonic period one cannot do better than study the paintings of General Baron Lejeune. Not only was he a most competent staff officer but also a more than competent artist. He was personally present at the battles which he portrayed, and his evidence of items comprising actual costumes is first class. This is not to say that every detail shown is beyond dispute, since no man's memory is infallible. (What Russian survivor of Stalingrad could remember now what he wore on any particular day of the siege?) Lejeune left eye-witness accounts, the beautiful neo-classical paintings that can now be studied in the Palace of Versailles. Two of Lejeune's paintings have been chosen for this book and certain details selected. In the painting of the Battle of Borodino between the French and the Russians in 1812, the foreground of the right section of the picture shows us typical French staff and cavalry uniforms of 1812 together with a few Russians. In such a picture the identification of the individuals and incidents and the units involved is almost a hobby in itself! The cuirassier style of the helmet with the flowing horse-hair tail was adopted by British dragoons and dragoon

Left: Russian Guardsman. Right: Italian foot carbineer

guards in 1812, but it was replaced by a modified form of the carbineer type after Waterloo, restored for a short time in the 1840s, and finally replaced by a metal version of the spiked helmet or *pickelhaube*. The French retained this cuirassier type, slightly modified, up to 1914, and indeed went to the First World War wearing it, with a khaki cover. The carbineer type was adopted in various armies after Waterloo, eg the British Life and Horse guards, dragoons and dragoon guards, Russian cuirassiers, etc. The last survivors of the carbineer type were in the Bavarian, *Chevaux-Légers* or possibly the 'Boston Blues' of the United States, who certainly wore them for the funeral of President McKinley in 1901.

Of those wearing the hussar costume in the Borodino picture, only one is wearing the fur cap known in the French service as a *kolpak*. The English word is 'busby', a word sadly misused by the press to describe the bearskin caps still worn by foot guards in Britain, Holland and Denmark. In most armies all the men in a cavalry regiment wore the same type of headdress, with the possible exception of musicians.

The élite companies

In the infantry it was not uncommon for the flank company – that is the grenadier company which took post on the right – and the light company, which took post on the left, to wear special headgear. In theory this was the bearskin for the grenadiers in the French and British services, but both tended to give them up on service. The grenadiers were the tallest men in the regiment and the light company small, active men for skirmishing. Both types were hand-picked. At one time it was the practice to collect the grenadier companies from all the regiments in a force into one unit, which weakened the regiments unduly. The custom developed of forming complete regiments of grenadiers, although this was now no more than a title of honour. The French extended this idea of an élite company to the cavalry, and in the hussars this company wore the fur cap as opposed to the *shakos* of the

remainder of the regiment. For a time some of the élite companies in the cuirassiers wore the bearskin, similar to grenadiers, in lieu of the helmet, a practice also extended to pioneers in dragoon regiments. The *Chasseurs-à-Cheval* or the Imperial Escort of the Guard were an élite regiment, and all ranks wore the fur cap (as on the figure seen from the back, at the foot of the birch tree in the Borodino picture).

Military musicians

Musicians were still much addicted to the cocked hat in the infantry and heavy cavalry, and it was common practice for the corps of drums and the musicians to be dressed in the colours of the regiment, but reversed. Thus a regiment dressed in blue with red facings might have musicians dressed in red with blue facings. However this was by no means always so; the *Chasseurs-à-Cheval* of the Imperial Guard had musicians dressed in sky blue and rose, although the regimental uniform was dark green and red. Sometimes the musicians were dressed the same as the rest of the regiment but with additional braid on collar, cuff and sleeve. The percussion instruments of the band – triangle, cymbals, etc – were of comparatively recent introduction in European armies, having been copied from the Turks during the eighteenth century, and it was in vogue to have men of colour dressed in outlandish costumes beating the kettledrums in the cavalry, or the cymbals in the infantry. The Garde Française had them at the time of the Revolution, and there were some in the British and Prussian services, but I have seen none in the Russian Army. Paradoxically, the musicians in the Indian native regiments of the Honourable East India Company at this time, and for many years to come, were Eurasians.

Of all non-commissioned officers none was or is still as magnificent as the Drum Major, upon whom the best that the corps or the government can offer has long been lavished. Taller headgear, larger epaulettes, more gold braid and higher plumes are the usual signs of this imposing figure. In the days when the regiments had their

Right: Hungarian infantryman. Far right: Italian officer of cuirassiers

own pioneers dressed in special uniform with apron and axe, the Drum Major headed the drums and the band immediately behind them. Now that pioneers no longer parade at the head of the regiment, the Drum Major leads the parade. So lavish did expenditure become in Napoleon I's cavalry on uniforms for the band, kettle-drum and trumpet banners that he cracked down and forbade such extravagance.

With the spread of French domination throughout Europe, French military fashions spread likewise amongst all allies and satéllites of the Empire. This sometimes makes identification extremely difficult. General officers (with exception of those specially appointed to a branch of the service, such as Colonel General of Dragoons) looked much alike in general pattern, the difference being mainly in colour; red for British, white for Austrians, etc. The Austrians had been the first to abolish the epaulette for all ranks. British generals did without them for twenty years, and then re-introduced them, the British Army as a whole losing them after the first Crimean War. Russian officers retained them up to the First World War in full dress, as did the Prussians, and the French still have them. In the French service the feathers round the hat brim were black for generals and white for marshals. In Bavaria, Austria-Hungary, and Great Britain the cocked hat remained in use for generals up to 1914. America abandoned it in the latter part of the nineteenth century, the Russians abandoned it by mid-century, while British staff officers retained it up to 1901 and generals up to 1914.

In the artillery, foot artillery tended to follow the fashions of the infantry, while horse artillery preferred the cavalry styles. Thus the French Horse Artillery of the Consular Guard, and later Imperial Guard, were full-blown sartorial hussars, whilst the British were only slightly less so; and the sole surviving horsed troop, the ceremonial King's Troop Royal Horse Artillery (called after King George VI), still wear the braided jacket as worn at Waterloo, almost unchanged. Other nations were not quite so exuberant. The drivers were considered somewhat socially inferior to the trained gunners, and were dressed

less resplendently. Napoleon III, however, dressed them better, if anything, and certainly his Train Drivers (these had nothing to do with locomotives!) were magnificently attired in grey, scarlet-trimmed hussar dress.

Extremes in fashion

After the final defeat of Napoleon I a general euphoria spread over Europe, and grateful sovereigns showered titles, orders and decorations upon all and sundry with prodigal abandon. So heavy a shower fell upon the great Duke of Wellington, victor of Waterloo, that it is said it took an hour and a quarter to read out all his titles and honours at his funeral. To complete the new and sparkling image of the conquering hero, new and sparkling uniforms were devised, which during the next two decades were to become so elegant, impractical and expensive that a general reaction against such extravagance was the natural outcome. But this was in the future. Immediately, the Allied armies were intermixing in Paris, eyeing each other's attire and doubtless assessing its comparative effect upon the female population. In Vienna the Congress brought together more sartorial ideas from all over Europe, providing an unparalelled feast, both financial and spiritual, for military tailors. The so-called First Gentleman of Europe, soon to be George IV of England, had samples of all manner of militaria sent for his inspection. Indeed it is said that this notable dandy was partly, if not wholly, responsible for the design of the superb new uniforms of the Maison du Roi which burst forth upon the astonished citizens of Paris (and the affronted Imperialists) almost before His (Restored) Majesty could dismount from his coach.

Immense headgear, tall plumes, tight jackets (in the 1820s the British Life Guards could not lift their arms above their heads to do the sword exercise) and tight-waisted full-bodied Cossack trousers were all the rage. The military costumes of this period seem to have more in common with the ballet or the (comic?) opera than with the grim business of war. This truly fantastic exuberance

9

Left: Bosnian infantryman. Right: Trooper of Italian light cavalry

repeated a phenomenon already encountered during the period of the Consulate, but some of the good taste to be seen in Philippoteaux's painting of the Battle of Rivoli, and the general sense of classical proportion, were missing; the vulgarity of design which was to symbolize the nineteenth century was, in this area at least, worse in these early decades than later on. However, none can deny the spectacular effect of these confections, and the pageantry of such an occasion as the Coronation Review of Queen Victoria in Hyde Park, London, in 1837.

Obviously this could not last. The crippling financial burden together with some inkling of the practical requirements of warfare combined to introduce some moderation. Soon a general upsurge of revolution throughout Europe was to introduce new ideas, spiced with the practical experience gained by the colonial powers in various parts of the world.

Practical simplicity

After their successes in North Africa the French found themselves the leading military nation in Europe once more. The practical good sense of their costume made a great impression, and the *képi* or French version of the *shako*, in all its various forms, was to spread to most armies from Russia to Mexico. The French Army was to have a new period of great sartorial magnificence under the Second Empire of Napoleon III, when they were once again the arbiters of military fashion. Latterly some simplification was adopted, as in the abolition of the pelisse for hussars; but all this was to go down before the spiked helmet or *pickelhaube* of the German states in 1870.

The greatest change of the mid-century was the introduction of the tunic in place of the cut-away tail coat. This was adopted by Prussians and allied states, Russian, French, and by the British after the Crimea. The outstanding feature of the earlier patterns was the remarkable fullness of the skirts. Gradually the tunic spread to all armies of Europe and the Americas, losing fullness in the process, and older styles of dress survived

only amongst the occasional guard unit, such as the Papal Swiss Guard or the Hungarian Noble Guard. Even such units as these usually adopted the convenient tunic for everyday wear, reserving their strange and ancient costumes for high days and holidays. The tail coat survived in one or two places, notably in the British Navy where it was official full dress for officers up to the Second World War.

The French Colonial costume of the Turco or Zouave was immensely popular in its day, although little trace now remains. When the Indian Army of the former Honourable East India Company was taken over by the Crown after the great Mutiny of 1857–58, the infantry was dressed in a modified form of this costume, a red coat with a false waistcoat of the regimental facing colour. In America some of the units adopted the fashion with wholehearted enthusiasm, eg the 5th New York Volunteers in the Union, and the First Louisianas in the South. Needless to say, once the war started and these costumes were worn out, they could not be replaced.

The French had a delightful notion of regimental *vivandières* in a modified form of the regimental uniform. Speculation is unlikely to cease as to what exactly were the functions and duties of these charming ladies. Possibly the trousers worn under the widespread skirts were introduced to allay the more scurrilous rumours. The 39th New York Volunteers, or Garibaldi Guards, who based their uniform upon another popular fashionable style, the Italian revolutionary Bersagliere, adopted the idea, and most fetching the lady looks in her scarlet and blue.

There appears to be some doubt as to whether Russia or Prussia first adopted the pattern of helmet which was to become famous as the *pickelhaube*. Once adopted the Prussians never abandoned it, whilst the Russians succumbed to the lure of the *képi* in the 1860s. But this lasted only a short time, for in 1882 Russia embarked upon her second attempt to create a military costume that was uniquely hers. This consisted of a double-breasted dark green coat with no visible buttons, of loose fit; loose breeches, and the long boots introduced in the 1860s. This

Russian officer of Circassian Cossacks

was to remain standard Russian uniform until the final attempt to smarten them up in 1911. Only the Imperial Guard units retained their traditional costumes of cuirassier, lancer, etc. All the line cavalry, more than forty regiments, was converted to dragoons in the new costume with various facings and a lambskin cap. This pattern was followed by the Bulgarian Army.

After the Franco-Prussian War of 1870 the spiked helmet was the fashionable military headdress, and the powers put their minds to adapting it to their needs. Some boldly adopted it as it was, altering only the insignia on the front, as in the Norwegian Infantry of the 1890s or the Hungarian Imperial Bodyguard. Others, notably the British and the Americans, adapted it, though whether with aesthetic or practical improvement is a matter of opinion. British Heavy Cavalry and Dragoons had already adopted a modified metal version before the Crimean War, and the Belgian General Staff adopted an anglicized version in the 1880s.

One of the most picturesque and popular uniforms of all time is that of Scots Highland regiments. This was an adaptation of the costume worn in the mid-eighteenth century when the Black Watch companies were raised to police the Highlands in the aftermath of the Jacobite rebellion of 1745. The wearing of the Highland costume was proscribed for civilians and only restored in the time of George IV in the early part of the next century. Originally armed with broadsword, musket, bayonet, dirk and target or shield, they eventually carried the same arms as the rest of British Infantry but the broadsword remains of Highland pattern still. Unlike the French *vivandières*, trousers were not worn underneath.

Uniforms of the Americas

Most European styles of uniform crossed the Atlantic to the Americas. In the north, military costume remained somewhat conservative, and it must be remembered that the United States governments were usually somewhat parsimonious and never kept up large quantities of

cavalry, and so, amongst the regulars at least, the opportunities for adopting extravagant uniforms did not exist. In the South, Argentina, Brazil and Mexico, for example, uniforms were devised as brilliant, dashing and impractical as anything to be found in Europe. Styles tended to get somewhat mixed, as in the Brazilian National Guard Hussars in the 1840s, who wore full hussar dress but with the Polish lancer cap, the trumpeters wearing a kind of heavy dragoon uniform with an enormous bearskin cap. In North America the lancer never really took on, and the one regiment in the Civil War with this arm, the 6th Pennsylvania Cavalry (Rush's Lancers) wore the normal cavalry uniform. The Hungarian hussar fur cap also failed to transplant until very late, and then not amongst the regulars; but the Kossuth hat, introduced by the Hungarian patriot in his tour to enlist aid for his fight against the Austrians, achieved an immense success, and became standard dress wear in the Northern Army and much favoured by cavalry in the South. For a time in the 1870s a very poor quality hat was used, and photographs are sometimes seen in which cavalry officers have twisted them into a cocked hat or *chapeau* giving an extraordinary old-world effect.

As far as I know the United States has never had a Presidential Guard unit, but citizens of that country have told me that they look upon the United States Marine Corps as fulfilling that role. In the 1840s the Marines had pure Second French Empire uniforms, the Drum Major wearing a fine hussar busby. The scarlet gold-braided coat is still worn, the busby being replaced by an enormous bearskin.

The French look of the US army survived through the Civil War and lasted until the replacement of the *képi* by the full dress helmet with spike or plume based upon the German *pickelhaube*, but in fact nearer to the British pattern. This headdress, with the cap lines looped to the chest by mounted men, and the plumes of matching colour which they wore, gave a very handsome albeit a more Prussian appearance. These helmets did not last long and at the turn of the century were replaced for full dress by

Left: French Zouave. Right: Grenadier of the German Fusiliers of the Guard

the peaked cap scarcely differing from the pattern worn today, except in colour. Much the same headdress is worn by all the armies of the European nations, and whilst most practical and comfortable it is not particularly elegant. It was not in the regular forces of the United States that the kaleidoscopic effect of European uniforms was to be seen, but in the militia or volunteer units. Before the First World War it was possible to find in these units most types from the 'Prussian Hussar' (New York Signals), British Dragoon, 1829 (Boston Blues) and a splendid variety of costumes of all periods. Some of these still survived between the World Wars.

The colonial influence

Not surprisingly the colonial powers of Europe were responsible for introducing their own ideas on military costume to their various colonies, occupied territories, protectorates etc, and they in turn were introduced to, or developed, ideas in these areas which became part of their national military costume. We have already seen how the French colonial troops in North Africa influenced fashion. Britain had long since established an army in India – or to be more accurate, three armies, since India was divided into three Presidencies, each with its own army: Bengal, Madras and Bombay. This vast empire was controlled by the Honourable East India Company up to 1858, and this must represent the largest private enterprise military (and naval) force ever established. Superb costumes of European pattern were inflicted on all and sundry, with little concession to the climate, at least in cut, although sometimes a light alpaca cloth was used. Later the use of cotton drill, white or khaki, and the lightweight sun helmet made life more bearable. The elegant and colourful uniforms in use up to 1857 owed nothing to oriental thought, except in the Irregular Cavalry and some of the Irregular Legions, or forces of mixed arms. These dressed in more suitable, loose clothing according to the whim of their commander. The officers in these corps were sometimes strangely clad in splendid oriental garments interspersed with occidental helmets, boots, etc, presenting a somewhat curious appearance. However the sensible and practical dress of the Irregulars, led usually by men of sound common sense whose minds were not completely hidebound, was the costume to survive up to 1914. Curiously, in the Indian Cavalry, officers retained an alternative style of European dress of lancer/hussar type; but in most regiments this was gradually replaced by the native style of dress, the European pattern being worn only upon rare full dress occasions when the officers were not on parade with the men. Eventually it became optional, although some regiments never abandoned it and in others officers never adopted the native style.

From India there were to come two notable contributions to military costume – the drab battle dress, khaki or mud colour; and the Sam Browne belt, universal symbol of an officer, as was once the gorget or vestigial piece of armour worn at the neck, or the sash. Khaki was widely used during the great Mutiny of the Bengal Army in 1857–1858 for obvious reasons of comfort, camouflage and ease of replacement. It proved so practical that by the end of the century it was standard service wear for the British Army. Surprisingly enough the red coat continued for a while on service, and the normal wear was a red frock coat or patrol jacket as worn in the Kaffir or Zulu Wars; and there were those who considered the moral effect of a red coat was worth half a dozen men. After the Great Mutiny, when the army could get down to proper peacetime soldiering, the forces in India were loath to return to even the modified form of their former finery now authorised. Witness this Order from Bombay Presidency Headquarters – 'Khaki uniform originally intended as a fatigue dress is more adapted to field service in the hot season than the respective cloth uniforms of the different arms, and as a general rule it must be restricted. The system of wearing it all seasons of the year is disapproved, as the practice has introduced into the army very slovenly habits, at variance with the proverbial correct and neat appearance of the officers and men of the British Army in India.'

Right: German *Jäger* in field order. Far right: German sapper

In May 1858 khaki was authorized in lieu of white for European regiments and in 1860 for native regiments for hot weather use only. Not all native regiments took advantage of this optional change, and many cavalry regiments continued to wear white as late as the 1880s, when white drill became the official hot weather full dress in the plains for the British Army in India, and remained so until 1914, while its use died out in the Indian Army.

The Russian Army also adopted a white hot weather uniform, in which it fought the disastrous Russo-Japanese War. The Japanese themselves, hurled from medieval feudalism into the modern industrial age within the previous 25 years, had simple blue uniforms of European style with gaiters and a peaked cap. Officers had adopted a French style braided jacket.

A farewell to colour

By the First World War the major powers had all adopted a more or less monochrome service uniform, with the exception of the French who clung to their traditional colours, although the cavalry covered metal helmets and breastplates with khaki cloth. This sort of thing was all very well for service, but the traditional regimental differences lingered on, and in the German Army the field grey service dress was as elaborate and of as good quality as full dress; and the hussars were looped and frogged, and lancers (uhlans) were be-plastroned, but all were in monochrome grey, enlivened here and there with coloured piping.

To modern minds it seems incredible that in the midst of the First World War, when the Hapsburg Emperor Franz Josef died in 1916, the state funeral was attended by such of the appropriate nobility, office holders of the Court and Empire, Palace Guards, etc, as could be present, all clad in the traditional magnificence of the ancient Hapsburg Empire. It was never to be seen again.

After 1919 nothing was ever the same again. Most of the old empires and monarchies had been swept away, and except for a very few élite guard corps, eg the British Household Cavalry and Foot Guards, or the French *Garde Républicaine*, the armies of Europe never returned to their former magnificence. The world was a different place: sartorial splendour was too expensive, and no longer fitted the image of the soldier the modern world required.

Sic transit gloria mundi.

Bibliography

In English
Martin, P. *Military Costume: A Short History of European Uniforms*, Herbert Jenkins, London 1965; Tudor Publishing, New York 1967. The edition with the text in English, French and German is particularly useful
Mollo, J. *Military Fashion*, Barrie & Jenkins, London 1972. Exceptionally good general work setting the historical stage in each period and with very fine illustrations
Kannik, P. *Military Uniforms of the World*, Blandford Press, London 1968; Macmillan, New York. A useful pocket-sized book with many colour plates
MacMunn, G. *The Armies of India*, A C Black, London 1912.

Rare but invaluable for the 1900–1914 period.
Tradition Monthly magazine on uniforms etc. Fine colour plates. 188 Piccadilly, London W1

In German
Knötel, R. *Handbuch der Uniformkunde*, Diepenbroick-Gruiter & Schulz, Hamburg; most recent edn. c. 1957. The classic primer; 1,600 monochrome illustrations

In French
Funcken, L. and F. *Le costume et les armes des soldats de tous les temps* (two volumes) 1967, *L'uniforme et les armes des soldats du Premier Empire* (two volumes) 1968, *L'uniforme et les armes des soldats de la Guerre 1914–1918* (two volumes) 1972. Casterman, Paris

French cuirass, Garde Royale, 1815. Gilt studs, shoulder straps and plaque; red lining, piped white, red belt and buckle.

Vice-Feldwebel, Fahnentrager, South West Africa c.1909, wearing gorget.

Glossary

Aiguillette, Aiglet, Aglet   cords, usually plaited, worn over the shoulder, the ends of which have either metal tags or tassels looped up to a button on the breast. Not to be confused with 'cap lines' (*q.v.*)

Bearskin   a cap made of this fur, and widely worn by grenadiers, eg Napoleon's Old Guard Grenadiers and British Footguards. It is *not* a busby although frequently referred to as such by the press.

Busby   the fur cap worn by hussars and *not* by British Footguards.

Cap lines   cords attached to a headdress and to the body of the wearer so that the headdress would not be lost if knocked off. The ends were often decorated with tassels or 'acorns'.

Cocked hat   a wide-brimmed hat with the brim 'cocked' or turned up. In the eighteenth century it was a tri-corne until about 1775 when it became a bicorne. Worn 'fore and aft' by Wellington and 'athwart' by Napoleon.

Cuirass   a breastplate, worn, for example, by British Lifeguards today in full dress.

Epaulette   shoulder strap, varying from a plain strap to most elaborate confections with metal crescents and fringe. Often used to denote rank. An alternative was the 'wing' worn over the point of the shoulder by, for example, bandsmen of the German Army.

Facings   name given to those parts of a uniform of a different colour, these usually being collar, cuffs, lining, as when lapels are left unfastened or turned back, etc. Thus uniforms of regiments in the British Army Lists were described as, eg 'red; Facings – green; Lace – gold'.

Dragoon   originally an infantry soldier trained to ride a horse well enough to get about, but supposed to dismount to fight as normal infantry.

Fusilier   an infantryman originally armed, in the seventeenth century, with a 'fusil' a lighter firearm than the contemporary musket. Latterly regiments were so called as an honour rather than because of any difference in equipment, although in most armies the headdress of fusilier regiments differed from that of the infantry of the line.

Hessian boots   short boots cut to a V shape in front and low at the back.

Gorget   armour worn around the neck. It survived in a vestigial decorative form long after armour was abandoned. In the British Army it was worn as the insignia of an officer of infantry on duty until 1831, and still is by standard bearers of the German Army.

Girdle   a band of material without tassels worn round the waist by, for instance, lancers and usually striped in two or more colours.

Grenadier   the name given to troops armed with grenades in the seventeenth century. A grenadier company was formed as part of an infantry regiment, taking post on the right flank, the light company of skirmishers on the left. During the Napoleonic Wars the practice of forming grenadier *regiments* spread, although the grenade itself was not in use any longer. The title eventually became one of honour rather than of tactical significance, although some differentiation from common soldiers was usually perceptible in their dress, eg the plumes worn by Prussian grenadier regiments in 1912.

Hussar   Light cavalryman after the Hungarian model; the braided dolman and fur edged pelisse were the features of Hungarian national dress most widely adopted.

14

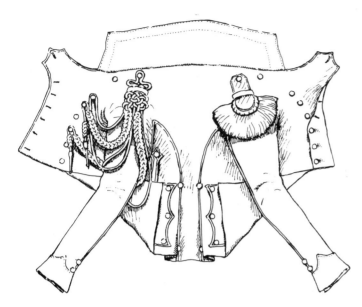

First French Empire. Lancer of the Vistula: no braid on the cuff; epaulette with six rows of white wool fringes and white straps on right shoulder; aiguillette on left shoulder.

Lancer after falling into disfavour during the seventeenth and eighteenth centuries the success of Napoleon's Polish Lancers and of the Cossacks heralded a revival of this arm, and the Polish costume of jacket with a plastron and the square topped cap were widely adopted.

Overalls trousers introduced during the Napoleonic Wars worn over the breeches and boots or gaiters to protect them. Later worn without the under garments.

Pelisse a jacket or coat after the Hungarian fashion, usually edged with fur and braided more or less heavily according to period. When it was not being worn it was carried slung over the left shoulder.

Pickers small spikes of metal worn on chains attached to the shoulder belt of cavalry officers in some regiments, and often shaped like arrows. Used originally for spiking the enemy guns, ie. inserting the spike in the touch-hole and breaking it off, so making it impossible to fire the gun.

Sabretache a sort of pouch or haversack originally worn by Hungarian horsemen, and later adopted widely by European cavalry as a despatch or map case; it was worn slung from the waistbelt and was often most elaborately embroidered.

Shabraque a saddlecloth.

Shako a peaked cap of Hungarian origin. Widely adopted by the military and varying enormously in shape and dimensions from the huge bell-topped models of the 1830s to the small compact pattern of the American Civil War or the French Army in 1914.

Sash usually worn by officers and sergeants as an indication, amongst others, of their rank.

Sword frog an attachment by which the sword is suspended closely to a waistbelt. Similar attachments are used for bayonets, etc.

Sword knot a strap attached to the sword which is meant to be worn round the wrist when the sword is in use to prevent it being dropped.

Sword slings straps by which the sword scabbard is attached to the belt.

1–2   Paintings of battles frequently contain fascinating details of military costume. Here we have the Battle of Borodino between the French and the Russians in 1812, painted by Baron Lejeune. His paintings are particularly interesting because he actually served with Napoleon's *Grande Armée*, and was therefore able to use first-hand knowledge and the sketches which he frequently made on the battlefield to reconstruct the scenes in his pictures. Many of the minor incidents portrayed are factual. In the detail at right a dying officer is attended by two members of his regiment while his pulse is taken by a senior medical officer; an *aide-de-camp* in hussar uniform hands him the cross of the Legion of Honour which Napoleon has sent him. Two dragoon officers (in dark green coats and brass helmets) form part of the group. On the right an infantry grenadier is guarding a Russian officer and some Kalmuk prisoners, and is kicking a live shell into a pool. In the centre of the right-hand picture Marshal Berthier, surrounded by a gaily-dressed staff, accepts the sword and surrender of General Sokeref. The Marshal is escorted by Red Lancers of the Guard; the lancers' double-breasted jackets could be folded back on each side and fastened in that position to allow the blue lining to show. Further in the background are infantry, advancing in their greatcoats; and over all, lit by the sun, the red-crested carbineers gallop forward, followed by cuirassiers in their distinctive steel breastplates. Advancing along a ravine in the left centre of the main picture are what appear to be *chevaux-légers lancier* in their lancer-style uniform and steel helmets which are a cross between those of the carbineers and the cuirassiers. At the extreme left of the main picture French infantry are seen in square formation, with another French marshal sheltering inside the square to the left of the regimental eagle.

3

4

5

Officier du Régim.t des Gardes Suisses, en petit uniforme.

6

7

8

3–8 The uniforms in these pictures illustrate the dramatic swing from the neat formality to be found in all armies at the close of the eighteenth century to the ragamuffin, *sansculotte* appearance of the French Revolutionary armies.

3 These are Danish officers of line infantry (left) and light infantry (right). The light infantry uniform is particularly interesting because it features the black and green combination favoured by rifle regiments in other countries. The tall, crowned headdress with its plume is a national peculiarity.

4 Volunteers of the City of London, of about 1803. Left to right: Mile End volunteer, Shoreditch volunteer, and Trinity Mineries volunteer. These costumes show the light infantry style of dress favoured by volunteer units throughout the United Kingdom. Notable are the Tarleton helmets of light dragoon pattern and the blue uniform, which in the British service was usually associated with the artillery arm.

5–6 A British sergeant of grenadiers of the 1st Foot Guards, and (centre) an officer of the French Swiss Guard. Here we have the formality of pre-Revolutionary military uniform in the tradition of Frederick the Great of Prussia. Like the Swiss Guard in this picture, the British foot guards wore long white gaiters on ceremonial occasions.

7 A French line infantryman of the early Revolutionary wars, which broke out in 1792. The most obvious distinctive feature is the big bicorne hat with its Tricolour cockade, but here is the basic pattern of French infantry costume which was to last throughout the Revolutionary and Napoleonic wars – the blue cutaway tail coat with white lapels, and the white crossbelts.

8 These are men of the ragged, threadbare Army of Italy which Napoleon took over in 1796 and led into the Po valley. To the amazement of Europe they defeated the well equipped and disciplined troops of the Austrian Empire in repeated battles. Note the wide variety of headgear – cocked hats, bearskins, and cloth caps – and the scruffiness of the trousers, often patched or made completely from any suitable material which could be acquired on the way.

10

11

9

9–12 A selection of cavalry uniforms from the period of the French Republic and the Consulate (1792–1804).

9 General Marchand, wearing the uniform of a light cavalry officer with a basic hussar pattern. The headdress is the *mirliton* with streamer, the streamer in this case being wrapped tight around the body of the headdress and not left floating loose, as in the officer facing Napoleon in **18** overleaf.

10 Here is an example of the full uniform of this type (and a back view is presented by the central figure on the facing page). This particular uniform was worn by troopers of the French dromedary corps formed during the French expedition to Egypt (1798–1801).

11 British cavalry costume of the period, in this case a volunteer of Lambeth Cavalry. Note the Tarleton helmet, as also worn by the London infantry volunteers in **4**.

12 French officers of the Consulate (1799–1804). The left-hand figure is an officer of dragoons, and the elegant brass helmet with its leopard-skin turban and black horsehair 'mane' is clearly shown. The back view of the officer of hussars in the centre shows the beautiful and elaborate embroidery common to this period, plus the sophisticated, silver-barrelled sash worn round the waist. Also notable is the headdress – a *shako* with plaited cords and tassels, and the scarlet cloth bag or 'fly' normally associated with the fur cap of the hussars. The right-hand figure of this group is the odd man out – a captain of infantry grenadiers (note the grenade emblem on the skirt of his coat). The tan-top, English-style hunting boots became all the rage in the French Army and were worn by infantry officers throughout the service down to Waterloo and after.

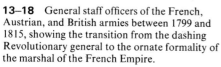

13–18 General staff officers of the French, Austrian, and British armies between 1799 and 1815, showing the transition from the dashing Revolutionary general to the ornate formality of the marshal of the French Empire.

13 General Kléber, who took over from Napoleon as commander of the French Army of Egypt in 1799. He wears the Tricolour sash, beautifully embroidered in gold by this time. His beautiful, oriental-patterned scimitar normally hangs at his left hip, hung over his right shoulder in a cord sling – also of oriental design.

14 A British *aide-de-camp* in full regalia. Notice the epaulettes and the elaborate gold embroidery on breast and cuffs, which is repeated on the tails of the coat.

15 In contrast to the *aide-de-camp*, this British general of infantry is shown wearing grey service trousers, embroidered coat without epaulettes, but with the gold aiguillette or twisted cord worn on his right shoulder.

16 An Austrian general of infantry, showing the simple style adopted early in the Austrian service, without epaulettes or any of the elaborate embroidery worn in the French and British services. The white coat remained the hallmark of the Austrian infantry for very many years. The soldier presenting arms at the left is a grenadier of line infantry in a German regiment, as opposed to the Hungarian regiments which wore blue pantaloons of Hungarian pattern.

17 Marshal Oudinot of Napoleon's *Grande Armée* in full dress uniform, wearing the heavily-embroidered dress coatee, gold sash, and the formal, classical-pattern sword reserved for ceremonial occasions. In his right hand he holds his blue velvet-covered, gold-mounted baton – the badge of office of a marshal. Napoleon's marshals frequently led attacks in person, and their uniforms made them conspicuous targets.

18 Napoleon at the Battle of Rivoli (1797). He wears a lavishly-embroidered general officer's uniform, with a richly-embroidered sword-belt over his Tricolour sash. The richness of his uniform and of the accoutrements of his fallen charger contrasts dramatically with his plain, 'English' hunting boots. Napoleon has just been re-horsed by a hussar officer who is handing him his hat. The hussar officer himself shows the back view of the dolman (jacket) and pelisse (fur-edged jacket slung over the left shoulder), plus the elaborate embroidery of the sabretache (the despatch-case slung from the sword-belt). Note also the *mirliton* headdress with its loose streamer. Later the wearing of gauntlets went out of fashion both for general officers and hussars.

19–20 Another painting by Baron Lejeune, this time of the Battle of Marengo between the French and the Austrians in 1800. The scene depicted is the dramatic moment when Napoleon's army was being driven from the field by the triumphant Austrians, and the last French division, 'marching to the sound of the guns', arrived just in time to counter-attack and save the day for the French. The section at left shows some interesting details of the French Consular Guard horse artillery, which is shown in action. The commander appears in the foreground beside the gun team, one horse of which has just been hit. In the rear one gun is in action. The uniform is basically that of light cavalry, and in fact under the Empire (1804–1815) the French horse artillery adopted the cavalry pelisse. Note that the drivers (one of whom is coloured) wear a different, simpler uniform to those of the gunners. In the background the Austrian forces are shown in considerable disarray as General Desaix's division counter-attacks at the left of the picture. Napoleon himself is shown at the left of the picture above, surrounded by a gorgeously-attired staff. And at the bottom left-hand corner an Austrian officer, unable to face the shame of defeat, raises a pistol to his head . . .

21

21   Before the French Revolution, a determined
series of army reforms gave France the best artillery
arm in Europe. This painting shows a French
artillery officer of about 1792, and apart from the
Tricolour cockade in the officer's hat it gives a good
idea of the sort of uniform worn by the young
Bonaparte when, after his time as an army cadet
on Royal Bounty, he was finally commissioned in
the artillery regiment of La Fère in 1785. Regular,
professional units like the French artillery arm
played a vital rôle in defending the infant French
Republic from the attacks of the armies of the
Ancien Régime – most notable at Valmy in
September 1792, when the sustained artillery
barrage of the Republican army under Dunouriez
was instrumental in saving France from invasion
by the Prussian army.

22   British counterpart: this portrait of Major-
General Sir Augustus Frazer of the Royal Horse
Artillery – although thoroughly romantic in its
conception and composition – shows the ornate
uniform worn by an officer of British horse artillery
during the Napoleonic wars. The basic headdress
was the fur-crested Tarleton helmet as worn by the
London volunteers in **4**, with a white plume. Note
the fur-lined, black-braided pelisse worn slung over
the shoulders.

22

23

23–26 Four groups depicting cavalry and infantry of the Army of Italy in Napoleon's heyday. Although these uniforms were worn by the army of the puppet Kingdom of Italy (of which Napoleon's stepson, Prince Eugene, was Viceroy), they are all basically of French pattern. The original army of Italy was purely a French force soldiering on the far side of the Alps; later it recruited Italians. The Italian troops of the Army of Italy put in a good deal of campaigning on Napoleon's behalf. Four of its divisions rushed to the Danube Valley in 1809 and were instrumental in winning Napoleon's victory over the

Austrians at Wagram; sizeable Italian formations shared the ordeal of the *Grande Armée* during the Russian campaign of 1812 and the retreat from Moscow. Many French trends – not only in uniform – were retained by the Italians after 1815.

23–24 These two groups have been selected from a larger print covering the cavalry of the Army of Italy. Above (foreground, left to right) are shown *gendarmerie* of the line and of the Royal Guard, dragoons from the Napoleon

24

25

Regiment and the Queen's Regiment, plumed chasseurs at centre right, and a driver of the engineer train.

24 The second group of Army of Italy cavalry shows (foreground, left to right): a driver of the army baggage train, an officer of horse artillery, a driver of the Royal Guard baggage train, and a dragoon of the *Garde d'Honneur*. The latter troops were special civic volunteers who were encouraged by Napoleon throughout the period of the Empire. They were permitted to adopt such

elaborate costumes as they chose – and were allowed the additional privilege of paying for them. At far right is a horse artilleryman of the Royal Guard.

25–26 A wide range of infantry uniforms from the Army of Italy, both guard and line regiments. Once again the overwhelming French influence in the design of military costume at this time is obvious. Of particular interest is the third figure from the left above, which shows the adoption by the Army of Italy of the helmet worn by the engineers of the French Imperial Guard.

26

27

28

29

27 An enormous guardsman is about to have his ears boxed by a diminutive officer, who is mounting a stool in order to reach his target. Both wear the dark, bottle-green uniform worn throughout the Russian service from this period onwards until the end of the nineteenth century. The laced stripes on collar and cuff indicate a guards regiment – a practice echoed by the uniforms of the Prussian Army. On the right an officer of heavy cavalry is flogging a soldier in undress uniform. The resigned expression on his victim's face suggests that the treatment lacks novelty.

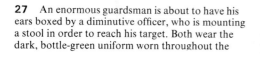

28 Another group of Russians of the 1815 period. On the left is a grenadier of the Preobrazhensky Guards with his mitre cap – a form of headdress which was already an historical anachronism but which survived until 1914. The officer in white is a cavalry officer of cuirassiers, standing behind an infantry officer wearing a *shako* headdress of peculiarly Russian pattern. Another cavalry officer, in undress uniform (whose aiguillettes seem to be coming adrift), is shaking hands with yet another infantry officer while a cossack rides past in the background.

29 From the Balkans at the time of Greece's fight for independence from Turkish rule – a soldier of Greek light infantry. His uniform is a confection of typically Balkan origin. Officers of this corps wore a superb helmet of classical pattern.

30 The classic uniform of a French regimental pioneer of the First Empire during the 'white-coat' period. It is said that the white coat was adopted by Napoleon's *Grande Armée* because one of the results of the British naval blockade was to cut off supplies of the indigo dye required to make the standard blue uniform cloth of the French Army. This situation did not last long (if only because suffering wounds in a white uniform was so demoralising) and the blue uniform was restored in about 1811. The pioneer's axe was not merely a ceremonial weapon: it was used for such practices as splitting logs or even, on occasion, skulls.

31 The plain, blue uniform worn (to their annoyance) by the French Imperial Guardsmen at Waterloo in 1815 is shown in this print of an 'Old Grumbler' who has accompanied Napoleon into exile.

30

31

32 Three superb cavalry uniforms of the *Grande Armée*. On the left is a cuirassier in full uniform, showing all the details of the classic cuirassier rig. The German Chancellor Bismarck was of the opinion that had these men been armed with lances they would have been the finest cavalrymen seen on the battlefield since the great days of the Byzantine Empire. In the centre is an officer of hussars. He wears the dolman unfastened over the braided waistcoat, and is not wearing the pelisse at all. (In winter the fur-edged pelisse could be worn buttoned-up as a jacket.) The hussar officer wears the leather-strapped overalls which were worn on service and common duties. In full dress, breeches and hessian boots were worn, and for gala wear the boots were often of crimson leather. The right-hand figure shows an officer of light cavalry, in this case of *chevaux-légers lancier* – a plain but most elegant uniform. He too wears the service overalls, which were basically a garment that could be buttoned up the sides and worn over the boots and breeches to protect them. In course of time the practice of wearing the boots and breeches beneath the overalls ceased.

33 Officers of the Prussian army of occupation in Paris, 1815, depicted by a French artist who was not completely overwhelmed with admiration. The left-hand figure shows the back view of an officer of cuirassiers, showing the Prussian adaptation of the crested helmet which certainly lacks the elegance of the French prototypes shown on the facing page. He is talking to a cossack officer employed in the Prussian service. In the centre is an officer of the famous Death's Head Hussars, who throughout their history were notable for their black uniform and their skull-and-crossbones badge. Beside him is an infantry officer of the light infantry of the Prussian Guard, and at the extreme right is a line infantry officer, wearing the undress cap which has since become almost universal.

34 The superbly barbaric costume worn by the kettle-drummers of the Polish Lancers of the French Imperial Guard. Under the First Empire, competition among cavalry regiments to have the most magnificent banners decorating the kettle-drums, not to mention the craze for sumptuous accoutrements in general, was so intense that Napoleon was forced to take a hand and forbid excessive expenditure on such luxuries.

35

36

35 French officers of the Bourbon Restoration, 1814–1815, when 'kings crept out to feel the sun'. Gorgeously-attired Royalist dandies, such as the ones shown here, caused much bitterness among the officers and men of the former Imperial army because of the favouritism shown them and the fact that they had seen little or no active service. At the left are two *Gendarmes du Roi* in dress and undress uniform. In the center is a Grey Musketeer in undress uniform. On the right a dragoon officer is shaking hands with a Grey Musketeer in full dress. The Grey Musketeer wears the emblem of the blazing cross – traditionally a musketeer symbol dating back to the seventeenth century and the days of Louis XIII and Cardinal Richelieu.

36 This print shows a selection of infantry uniforms of the Prussian Army of about 1815. Left to right: an *Unteroffizier* in parade uniform, a *Gemeiner* or private in marching order (notice the waterproof covering on his *shako*), a bandsman, and a *Landwehr* infantryman being inspected by an officer in parade dress. All these uniforms are notable for their practical simplicity; note the combined gaiters and trousers – white for summer, grey for winter.

37 Another exotic confection from the French Royalist Army of 1815 – this time a trumpeter of cuirassiers of the *Garde Royale*.

38–39 British 'Regency period' flamboyance taken to its extremes. The left-hand figure in **38** is an officer of the 1st Regiment, Grenadier Guards – in undress uniform. He stands beside an officer of the 2nd Regiment, Coldstream Guards, in full dress. The officer in **39** is of the 23rd Light Dragoons (Lancers) in 1817. His *schapka* headdress, originally of Polish design, is typical; the *schapka* became extremely popular with British lancer regiments.

37

39

40–44 The musicians – some military bandsmen of the period 1800–1850.

40 A magnificent detail of an Italian military band of about 1800 – brass and woodwind. Propped against the drum at bottom right is the 'Jingling Johnny' – a standard hung with many small bells of Turkish origin, still carried in the German Army.

41 A detail from a painting of the 2nd British Life Guards at Windsor in 1830, showing the magnificent costume of the kettle-drummers. This exotic uniform did not endure for long. The normal state dress is shown by the figures on the left, mounted on white horses.

42–43 Bandsmen from the Saxon Army which fought beside Napoleon's *Grand Armée*.

42 An infantry drum major – by tradition one of the most gorgeously attired personalities in any army of the period – with two drummers.

43 A trumpeter of heavy cavalry, an artillery bandsman, an infantry bandsman, and a trumpeter of transport.

44 Across the Pyrenees – a drum major, a trumpeter, and a drummer of Spanish infantry, of about 1840.

45

45–48 Doctors and others – a selection of uniforms from the Russian, French, and British armies of the nineteenth century.

45 With the Russian Army medical corps of about 1830. An incapacitated officer of lancers, with his personal equipment held by two members of the medical corps, is taken in charge by a regimental surgeon.

46 A French veterinary officer (left) and a medical officer, both in full dress, of about 1870.

46

47 A selection of officers from various service corps of the British Army. The mounted officer in the cocked hat is a Commissary General; beside him, also mounted, is a Deputy Assistant Commissary General. The left-hand officer on foot, wearing the cocked hat, is an Inspector General Surgeon of Hospitals, with a Surgeon on the Medical Staff beside him. The two officers on the right are a Veterinary Surgeon, 1st Class (with red plumes), and an Assistant Commissary General of Ordnance.

48 The pomp of power. This haughty officer, bowling along in his personal transport, is a Russian staff surgeon.

COMMISSARY GENERAL.   DEPUTY ASS^T COM^{SY} GENERAL

INSPECTOR GENERAL   SURGEON   STAFF PAYMASTER   ASS^T COM^{SY} GENERAL   VETERINARY SURGEON
SURGEON OF HOSPITALS   MEDICAL STAFF   OF ORDNANCE.   1ST CLASS

47

48

49

50

51

52

53

54

49 An officer of the Hungarian Noble Guard, in full dress. This high-ranking unit of the Austro-Hugarian Empire survived until the fall of the Hapsburgs in 1918. This uniform dates from about 1800.

50 Swiss Papal Guard of 1828, in undress uniform. The basic uniform of the Swiss Guard dates back to Renaissance times, but the headdress of this period is of contemporary Austrian pattern – a reminder of the strong Austrian influence in northern Italy, large areas of which were under Austrian rule at this time.

51 Two more exotic uniforms of 1831, worn by Polish volunteers. After a brief emergence as the 'Grand Duchy of Warsaw'– a creation of Napoleon – Poland passed under Russian rule in 1815. This, however, had little or no effect on the strong Polish influence on military costume.

52 Officer of the Belgian Civil Guard, 1831. This uniform also features the very full-skirted frock coat favoured by the Poles.

53 Pioneers of infantry from the Spanish Army, with the figure on the right in undress uniform. Spanish military fashions of this date – 1842 – are notably French in origin and have a look of the early French 2nd Empire.

54 Two Russian guardsmen: on the left is a non-commissioned officer of the Pavlovsky Guards, with a drum major (in a magnificent, heavily-braided tunic) of the Preobrazhensky Guards on the right. Both date from around 1854 and the outbreak of the Crimean War – one of the last European wars when full dress was worn on the battlefield.

55 An officer of the Milan Civic Guard, about 1850.

56   A French gunner of the 2nd Empire, about 1850. Notice the braided dolman and fur cap inherited from the styles of the 1st Empire.

57   A startling return to informality in military costume was made by the Italian freedom-fighter Garibaldi and his Redshirts, here shown defeating regular Neapolitan troops in the Battle of Calatafimi in 1859. The red shirt, combining practicality, comfort, and emphatic romantic appeal, was adopted as far away as the United States, where one unit in the early Civil War called itself the 'Garibaldi Guards'. The uniforms of the unfortunate Neapolitans in the picture reflect a strong French influence.

58   Once again, the stamp of the French style, this time on the uniforms worn by two Spanish foot artillerymen of about 1842.

59   Piedmontese *Bersaglieri* in action at Custoza in 1849, with the plumed hats which these élite troops were to make famous.

60   Regular Piedmontese infantry in the Battle of Novara in 1849 make a last stand against the Austrians under Radetzky.

61   British troops attacking the Sikh army at Moodkee in 1845. Apparently the only concession made to the climate is the white linen cover over the cap. The high collars and leather stocks might well be considered unsuitable for warfare in India, but only in the hot season – and Moodkee was a winter battle. Within a few years a battle dress of simple cut and lightweight material was to originate with the use of khaki-dyed drill during the Great Mutiny. At bottom left is a Sikh infantryman in British-style uniform.

60

61

62–65 Selected cavalry uniforms of the mid-nineteenth century.

62 The elegant costume of Russian heavy cavalry, in this case cuirassiers of the Tsarevitch Regiment. At far left an officer in full dress chats with a brother officer in undress uniform while a trumpeter holds the horse. The red plume of the trumpeter reflects the practice common throughout Europe of marking out bandsmen and musicians with coloured plumes – often, indeed, with entirely different uniforms of their own.

63 Beautiful full-dress uniform of an officer of Madras Light Cavalry. It is said that the French-grey colour of this uniform was introduced because the Honourable East India Company found itself with a surplus of this material, and decided to use it to clothe its cavalry.

64 An officer of Cape Mounted Rifles, 1864. This shows the attractive rifle uniform – dark green with black lace – as worn by officers.

65 A mounted grenadier of the Russian Imperial Guards, about 1850. This style of cap, first introduced for a short period in the eighteenth century, survived unaltered until 1914.

OFFICER OF THE CAPE MOUNTED RIFLEMEN.
1842.

64

63

65

43

66

68

67

69

44

66–71 General and staff officers of the mid-nineteenth century.

66 British staff officers in service dress during the siege of Mooltan in the Sikh Wars. Notice the variety of headdress, and the long cap covers used to keep the sun off the back of the neck.

67 A British *aide-de-camp* to the Sovereign of the 1830s – full dress uniform.

68 Marshal Grouchy, of Waterloo fame, in full dress. A comparison with Marshal Oudinot in **17** shows the change in the uniform of French marshals after 1815.

69 King Frederick William III of Prussia, wearing the sombre general officer's uniform of the Prussian Army after Waterloo.

70 Austrian general staff officers in the field during the suppression of the Vienna Revolution of 1848. The general and staff officers can be identified by their dark green plumed cocked hats. A variety of other uniforms is also present, most notably the extreme length and fullness of skirt of the hussar officer's pelisse at centre left, with the wearer speaking to a general officer in a red-lined coat.

71 A Russian *aide-de-camp* to the Tsar. He is a contemporary of the British *aide-de-camp* opposite, and there are many striking similarities in the richness and detail of their uniforms.

71

72

72–75 Indian colonial troops of the nineteenth century.

72 An officer of Dutch Bengal Lancers. He wears the typical European-style lancer uniform of the 1830s, while his *sowar* or native cavalryman wears a splendid oriental costume which contrasts strongly with **73**.

73 A sepoy or native cavalryman of the Honourable East India Company. Unlike the *sowar* in the picture above, his uniform follows the style of European light cavalry of the period, but with a distinctive turban.

74 A camel *zamburak* or 'light gun', fixed to the camel saddle by a swivel mounting, is being fired by a *sowar* of the Hyderabad Native Cavalry. His uniform is in effect the classic irregular cavalry dress of the period – about 1845, twelve years before the Great Mutiny.

75 An officer of the 6th Irregular Cavalry of the Bengal Army. His uniform is typical of the magnificent cavalry costumes which officers of irregular colonial units sometimes permitted themselves. It certainly contrasts sharply with the simple dress of his men in the background.

73

74

75

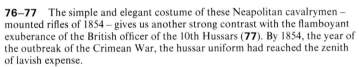

76–77 The simple and elegant costume of these Neapolitan cavalrymen – mounted rifles of 1854 – gives us another strong contrast with the flamboyant exuberance of the British officer of the 10th Hussars (**77**). By 1854, the year of the outbreak of the Crimean War, the hussar uniform had reached the zenith of lavish expense.

78 Officer of British heavy cavalry – the 2nd (Queen's) Dragoon Guards – has a basic simplicity, apart from the enormous bearskin crested helmet which became popular in the 1830s.

79

80

82

79 A *havildar* or sergeant of an Indian mountain artillery battery, about 1900. Note the puttees or cloth leg wrappings making their first appearance.

80 Three native infantrymen of the Madras Army, about 1850, showing winter and summer dress. Left to right: an infantry company sergeant, a grenadier, and a centre company sepoy or native soldier. The figure at extreme left is a regimental cadet – a boy who would be born into a regiment, grow up with it, and eventually enlist himself.

81 Commandant of the Bikanir Camel Corps, 1813 – a famous unit which still survives today.

82 Officers and men of the Indian Army, about 1890. Back row, mounted, left to right: a *sowar* of Central India Horse; a British officer of the Corps of Guides (Queen's Own); a *sowar* of the 3rd Bengal Cavalry; a British officer of the 6th Punjab Infantry; a *sowar* of the 13th Bengal Lancers (Duke of Connaught's Own); a British officer of the Viceroy's Bodyguard; a native officer of the Corps of Guides; a *sowar* of the 3rd Madras Light Cavalry; a camel *sowar* of the 10th Bengal Lancers; a *sowar* of the Viceroy's Bodygyard; and a *sowar* of the 3rd Bombay Lancers. Front row, on foot, left to right: a native officer of the 4th Madras Light Cavalry (Prince of Wales' Own); a native officer of the Queen's Own Madras Sappers and Miners; a native officer of the 14th Bengal Lancers; a native officer of the 1st Bombay Lancers; a sepoy of the 20th Bengal (Punjab) Native Infantry (Duke of Cambridge's Own); a sepoy of the 2nd Goorkhas (Prince of Wales' Own); and a sepoy of the 15th Bengal Native Infantry (Loudianah Sikhs).

83 *Turcos* or native soldiers of the French colonial army in Algeria. This style of uniform also became popular in the United States in the early Civil War.

83

49

84

85

86

84–85–87 Legacy of glory: uniforms of the French 2nd Empire, deliberately modelled on the splendours of the Napoleonic army. This imitation applied to uniform details of all arms – whether the white plastron of the *voltigeur* or light infantryman (**84**), the light infantry uniform of the Guard (**85**) or the braided tunic of the trumpeter of cuirassiers (**87**).

86 The light, comfortable style of uniform adopted by British volunteers raised throughout Great Britain during the early period of the French 2nd Empire as a result of fears that the French intended to invade England. These are rifle volunteers of about 1860.

88 A lieutenant (left) and a staff officer of the
United States Marine Corps, both of the nineteenth
century. The US Marine Corps was voted into
existence by Congress in the spring of 1798, when
the young Republic was facing the threat of a war
with France and was anxious to raise a regular unit
which could serve either on shipboard or on land
as regular infantry. The US Marines soon earned
themselves a reputation second to none as a tough
combat unit which would always manage to hold a
bridge-head for the army troops which followed.
Like the US Army of the period, the US Marine
Corps of the nineteenth century was soberly
conventional in its uniform: massive epaulettes,
sober, navy-blue tunic and trousers, and the
distinctive, double row of heavy brass buttons
down the front.

89 Officers of the United States Army of the
period 1832–1835. The officer in the centre, holding
his sword under his left arm, is a major-general. He
is surrounded by staff officers and officer cadets.

90 Uniforms of the army of the Confederate
States of America, set up during their fight for
independence from United States Federal rule
which erupted into civil war in 1861. From left to
right: an infantry captain, an artillery colonel, a
general, a cavalry sergeant, a cavalry trooper (in
cape, mounted), an infantryman (in cape, on foot),
an infantryman in basic dress, and a corporal of
artillery. Apart from the far more attractive,
medium-grey colour of the Confederate uniform,
the Confederate States Army adopted many of
the rank badges and colour differentiations of the
US Army. Many Confederate officers had held
commissions in the US Army up to the outbreak of
the Civil War; and the most famous of them,
Robert E. Lee, had in fact been offered the
command of the Union Army before he decided
that 'I am a Virginian' and rode south to the
Confederacy.

91 American Civil War uniforms of the United
States Army. In the Civil War the US Army
retained the basic dark-blue uniform, rank being
shown by shoulder and arm badges. Left to right:
an officer wearing the greatcoat (mounted), an
infantry corporal, a lieutenant-colonel (mounted),
an infantry sergeant, an infantry private soldier
in marching order, an infantryman wearing the
cape, and an infantry officer in field uniform. Owing
to the infinite superiority of the US Army's
supply facilities in the Civil War, the uniforms
shown here are accurate representations of the
costume which would be actually worn in the
field. In the Confederate Army very few soldiers
retained much of their official uniforms after the
first year of the war. Like the soldiers of the French
Revolutionary army, they tended to kit themselves
out in any available clothing they could find.

92 Staff and line officer of the United States
Army of 1888 in full dress; the seated figure in the
plain black costume is an army chaplain. Note the
considerable changes in staff officers' uniform
since the 1835 period, represented in **89**, particularly
the appearance of the double-breasted frock coat
instead of the cutaway tail coat. The plumed helmet
worn by the officer on the right is similar in its
basic pattern to the helmet worn by the British
Army of the time.

93 A mounted officer of cavalry talks with a
signal corps sergeant, whose service distinction
is the orange colour of his helmet plume and cord.
This picture is particularly interesting because it
shows one of the negro cavalry regiments of the
US Army which were exceptionally fine regiments.
At this period, 1880, the somewhat sombre
appearance of the American regular forces was
offset by the frequently exotic confections of
militia or volunteer units.

94

94–97 German Empire uniforms of 1871, from Prussia, Württemberg, and Saxony.

94 Officers and men of the Prussian guards cavalry regiments. Left to right: staff officer of Guards Cuirassiers; lieutenant of the *Garde du Corps* in full dress; trooper of Black Cuirassiers; lieutenant of Guards Lancers; trooper of Guards Lancers in parade dress; trumpeter of Guards Dragoons in parade

dress; lieutenant of Life Guard Hussars; staff trumpeter in winter uniform.

95 From the Kingdom of Württemberg. Left to right: major-general in parade dress; lieutenant-general; general *aide-de-camp* to the King; non-commissioned officer of the Palace Guard in parade dress; *aide-de-camp* to the King; adjutant (lieutenant of the 1st Württemberg) in parade dress; a staff major; and a lieutenant-colonel of the General Staff in parade dress.

95

96 Prussian *Jäger* (riflemen) and light infantry. Left to right: a *Hauptmann* (captain) of Guards Jäger in parade dress; a Guards Rifleman, in parade dress; a musician of the 6th Silesian *Jäger*; rifleman of the 2nd Pomeranian *Jäger* in greatcoat and marching order; orderly of the 14th Mecklenburg *Jäger*; sergeant of the *Leib-Gendarmerie* in the full dress worn when in attendance on the King of Prussia; orderly on the staff of the Prussian VI Army Corps; a lieutenant of mounted *Feldjäger* in *pickelhaube* helmet and top coat.

97 Cavalry uniforms from the Kingdom of Saxony. Left to right: a lieutenant of Guards cavalry in palace uniform; a trumpeter of carbineers (2nd Heavy Regiment) in full dress; a lancer of the 2nd *Ulanen*, 18th Regiment, in full dress; an *unteroffizier* of the 1st *Ulanen*, 17th Regiment, in undress uniform; a lieutenant of the 2nd Hussars, 18th Regiment (*Kaiser Friedrich, König von Preussen*), in full dress; a hussar in basic uniform (note the carbine as well as the sabre); a hussar in field dress; and a regimental sutler of cavalry.

99

98–101 Contrasts in cavalry uniforms of the British and Russian armies at the end of the nineteenth century. The clean simplicity of the cavalry sergeant-major at left contrasts equally strongly with the outlandish appearance of his immediate predecessors at bottom right and the colourful variety of the British cavalry uniforms above.

98 A Russian dragoon sergeant-major of about 1890.

99 'Our British Cavalry, 1890'– a brilliant selection of principal cavalry uniforms in the last decade of the century. Background, left to right: A trooper of the 16th Lancers; a trooper of the 4th Dragoon Guards (on foot); a trooper of the 2nd Life Guards; a trooper of the 18th Hussars; an officer of the 13th Hussars; a trooper of the 12th Lancers (back view); an officer of the 10th Hussars; a trooper of the 7th Dragoon Guards; a trooper of the 4th Hussars; a trooper of the 2nd Dragoon Guards (Queen's Bays); and a trooper of the 7th Hussars. Foreground, left to right: a trooper of the 3rd Hussars; a sergeant of the 15th Hussars; an officer of the 11th Hussars; an officer of the 6th Dragoon Guards (Carabiniers); an officer of the 1st Life Guards; an officer of the 14th Hussars; an officer of the Royal Horse Guards; an officer of the 5th Dragoon Guards; an officer of the 5th Lancers; an officer of the 2nd Dragoons, Royal Scots Greys; a corporal of the 1st Royal Dragoons; and a trooper of the 17th Lancers.

100 Glittering anachronism: an officer of Circassians of the Tsar's escort, reminiscent more of the Byzantine Empire than of the nineteenth century.

101 Russia's crack cavalry were the Cossack regiments, deadly with both lance and sabre – and, by 1914, with the rifle as well. The figure on the left is a warrant officer of artillery of the Cossacks of the Guard, while the mounted trooper is a Cossack of the Guard.

98

102

102–106 A salute to the ladies. We are not concerned here with those numerous historical examples of women who have masqueraded as soldiers, but with the rather pleasant conceit of women wearing military costume. There are eye-witness accounts from the Napoleonic wars of the discovery on the battlefield of the corpses of young women who had followed their lovers to battle and death, sometimes dressed in superb hussar uniforms. In the 2nd French Empire regimental *vivandières* (canteen girls) were attired in a variation of the regimental uniform and presented a most picturesque appearance. The young woman in **103** dates from the beginning of our period – 1789 – when during the great period of Revolutionary enthusiasm in France innumerable patriotic processions and pageants were staged in the name of liberty, and both sexes would do pike-drill to demonstrate their eagerness to die for the country.

102 The Crown Princess of Rumania in elegant hussar rig as Colonel-in-Chief of the *Rosiori* or Red Hussars.

103 Patriotic ardour: a French girl of the time of the Revolution, proudly wearing the Tricolour colours, marching out for drill on the Champ de Mars in Paris.

104 This representation of Queen Victoria on horseback is a Gothic Revival fantasy, but on several occasions Queen Victoria did appear in a modified form of military costume – as does her great-granddaughter, Queen Elizabeth II, for the ceremony of the Trooping of the Colour every year.

105–106 Two of the charming *vivandière* uniforms as favoured by heavy and Guards light cavalry of the 2nd French Empire.

103

Jeune Francaise allant au Champ de Mars faire l'Exercice

Cuirassiers.

105

104

Victoria I. Königin von England.

Chasseurs de la garde à cheval.

106

107

10

108

107–108 Two Highlanders of the nineteenth century. The first Highland regiments were raised after the English conquest of the Highlands which crushed the last great Jacobite uprising in 1745, and they soon established a fighting reputation second to none. Their kilts were highly distinctive, but they could cause mild consternation, as in 1815 when the British supplied troops for the Allied Army of Occupation in France. The lady of one house in which Highlanders were billeted commented in amazement: '*C'est vrai! Actuellement, rien qu'un petit jupon!*'

107 A Highland officer of the mid-nineteenth century, in full regalia. Note the ostrich feathers in his bonnet, and the goatskin sporran – reputedly a military variation on the simple leather purse,

very necessary for Highland dress as the kilt has no pockets. His regiment is the 78th (Highland) or Rosshire Buffs.

108 A soldier of the Queen's Own Cameron Highlanders of about 1890. Notice the evolution of the bonnet, which developed from stiffening a basic, beret type of headdress into a 'pork-pie' shape, and adding more and more ostrich feathers over the years until nothing but the chequered border of the cap was visible.

109 British artillery in action during the Battle of Colenso in the Boer War (1899–1902). Here is the basic pattern of the new-style service dress: drab khaki throughout, on jacket, breeches, and puttees.

110 A British infantryman in tropical service dress, typical of the end of the nineteenth century.

111 A Sikh officer of the same period, showing the adaptation of native dress to field service. Note the steel ring worn over the turban – an item of adornment which could be used as a lethal weapon.

112–113 'Tommy Atkins' goes to war – the British khaki field dress at the time of the outbreak of the First World War in 1914.

112 Trumpeter of the Royal Horse Artillery.

113 Field service dress of the Queen's Own Royal West Kent Regiment. The officer on the left wears his badge of rank on the cuff – the practice in the British service at this time.

110

111

112

113

61

114

115

114 This unusual uniform of mounted rifles – the only one of its kind in the British Empire in 1900 – shows a unit of volunteer cavalry of yeomanry: the East Kent Mounted Rifles. A number of these regiments existed throughout the British Isles, their uniforms varying from pelissed hussars of 1850 style to dragoons and lancers.

115 British general and staff officers, 1865–1870. Left to right: an *aide-de-camp* to the Queen; a general; a major-general of artillery; a general's *aide-de-camp*; an *aide-de-camp* to the Queen (militia); a field-marshal; an *aide-de-camp* to the Queen (artillery); a colonel (unattached; holding the stated rank but without a specific appointment); a lieutenant-general; a general of hussars; orderlies of the 5th Lancers; an adjutant-general; a brigade major; an inspector-general of hospitals; and an *aide-de-camp* in undress uniform. To wear the uniform of the general officer of hussars, special permission had to be obtained from the Queen. It is interesting to note that the young man in the uniform of a colonel, unattached, represents Edward, Prince of Wales – later King Edward VII.

116 De-glamourising the image of the glittering general: Lieutenant-General Sir H.M.L. Rundle in drab khaki service dress, complete with tropical helmet, and wearing the now-ubiquitous 'Sam Browne' belt.

117 Field-Marshal Sir Garnet Wolseley, Commander-in-Chief of the British Army, wearing the full-dress uniform of a British field-marshal with all his orders and decorations, and holding his baton.

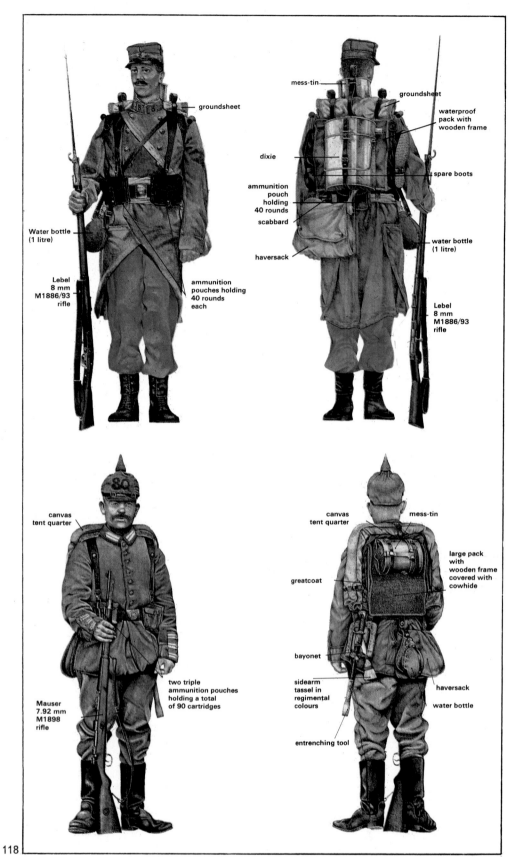

groundsheet

Water bottle (1 litre)

Lebel 8 mm M1886/93 rifle

ammunition pouches holding 40 rounds each

mess-tin

groundsheet

waterproof pack with wooden frame

dixie

spare boots

ammunition pouch holding 40 rounds

scabbard

water bottle (1 litre)

haversack

Lebel 8 mm M1886/93 rifle

canvas tent quarter

Mauser 7.92 mm M1898 rifle

two triple ammunition pouches holding a total of 90 cartridges

canvas tent quarter

mess-tin

greatcoat

large pack with wooden frame covered with cowhide

bayonet

sidearm tassel in regimental colours

haversack

water bottle

entrenching tool

118

119

120

118 Rivals of 1914: French and German infantrymen. After the disaster of the Franco-Prussian War of 1870 when the 2nd French Empire was overthrown by the Prussian invasion, the French Army deliberately retained its colourful and distinctive uniform. The *pantalon rouge* was regarded as an essential aid to morale – but the first French offensives of 1914 proved that in the age of the machine-gun it made its wearer a fatally obvious target. The German infantryman was already dressed in far less conspicuous *feldgrau* or field grey, with his *pickelhaube* shielded with a cloth cover on which his unit number was displayed.

Notice that even in service dress the stripes of the German guards regiments, which formed so conspicuous a part of the full-dress uniform, were faithfully retained on collar and cuff.

119–120 Military uniform adapts to the needs of trench warfare. The French *poilu* of the time of Verdun (1916) wears the neutral, *horizon bleu* greatcoat, tunic, breeches, and puttees, and the steel helmet has made its appearance. The basic German uniform has remained unchanged apart from the distinctive, 'coal-scuttle' helmet and the addition of a gas mask.